Troubadours

dieval music to sing and play

selected and edited by

BRIAN SARGENT

Keswick Hall College of Education, Norwich

CAMBRIDGE UNIVERSITY PRESS

The Resources of Music Series

General Editors: *Wilfrid Mellers, John Paynter*

1 THE RESOURCES OF MUSIC *by Wilfrid Mellers*
2 SOUND AND SILENCE *by John Paynter and Peter Aston*
3 SOMETHING TO PLAY *by Geoffrey Brace*
4 MUSIC DRAMA IN SCHOOLS *edited by Malcolm John*
5 THE PAINFUL PLOUGH *by Roy Palmer*
6 THE VALIANT SAILOR *by Roy Palmer*
7 TROUBADOURS *by Brian Sargent*
8 MINSTRELS *by Brian Sargent*
9 POVERTY KNOCK *by Roy Palmer*

Acknowledgements

Full source references to songs and prose passages are given on pages 39–40. Sources of illustrations are listed on p.40. The author and publisher would like to thank all those there listed for permission to reproduce material in this book.

While every effort has been made to contact copyright holders, the publishers apologise if any material has been included without permission.

Performing and recording rights are reserved and are administered by the Performing Rights Society, The Mechanical Copyright Protection Society and the affiliated bodies throughout the world. Applications should be made to these bodies for a relevant licence. Failure to so apply constitutes a breach of copyright.

Front cover: Musicians play a wind instrument and a drum. The title page picture shows a portative organ. Both illustrations are from a thirteenth-century Spanish manuscript.

CAMBRIDGE UNIVERSITY PRESS
Cambridge, New York, Melbourne, Madrid, Cape Town, Singapore, São Paulo, Delhi, Tokyo, Mexico City

Cambridge University Press
The Edinburgh Building, Cambridge CB2 8RU, UK

Published in the United States of America by Cambridge University Press, New York

www.cambridge.org
Information on this title: www.cambridge.org/9780521204712

First published 1974
Re-issued 2011

A catalogue record for this publication is available from the British Library

Library of Congress Catalogue Card Number: 73-93396

ISBN 978-0-521-20471-2 Paperback

Contents

Introduction   *page*   4

  1 A la fontenele (In the river valley)   8

  2 (a) A l'entrade del tens clar (When the spring comes)   10

      (b) Veris ad imperia   11

  3 Au tans d'aoust (Autumn is coming)   14

  4 Bergier de ville champestre (Shepherds work high) by Robert de Rains   15

  5 Bergeronnete (Let's celebrate together) by Adam de la Halle   16

  6 Der Kuninc Rodolp (King Rudolph) by Der Unvürzaghete   18

  7 Dy mynne ist gut (My cottage is damp) by Reinmar von Zweter   20

  8 Nu huss! (Attack!) by Oswald von Wolkenstein   21

  9 Foy porter (Don't be stern) by Guillaume de Machaut   22

 10 Fulget hodie (Brightly shines today)   24

 11 Omnes gentes, plaudite (All you people)   25

 12 Orientis partibus (What a fine and splendid beast!)   26

 13 O Roma nobilis (O great and glorious Rome)   30

 14 Prendés i garde (I'm after trout) by Guillaume d'Amiens   32

 15 Quand je voi (When winter winds come) attrib. Colin Muset   33

 16 Qui creavit coelum (He who made the heavens)   34

 17 Veníte a laudáre (O come with praises ringing)   35

 18 Winder wie ist nu dein kraft (Winter, gone is all) by Neidhart von Reuenthal   36

Suggestions for further activities   37

Sources   39

Index of Songs   40

Introduction

Over the past few years there have been signs of an increasing interest in medieval music. Recitals of attractive and colourful examples from the period are now quite common, and numerous ensembles have been formed for their performance. The number of people for whom the expression 'medieval music' conjures up the prospect of a dreary and forbidding mystery is steadily diminishing.

In the field of so-called 'educational music' the pioneer work of Ralph Dunstan and Christopher Bygott in *Musical appreciation through song* (Schofield & Sims, 1922), which incorporated several examples of medieval music, was, as far as I know, alone until relatively recently. Now, however, one may see evidence of the growing interest in music of this period in recent publications and also for example in BBC music programmes for schools. Even so, some of its potentialities for school use remain untapped, and this book is an attempt to remedy the neglect.

It is all too easy to forget that what we sometimes casually call medieval music can cover a vast stretch of some 600 years, from approximately the beginning of the ninth century to at least the end of the fourteenth, in other words, a period longer than that from AD 1400 to the present day. If one thinks of the developments which have taken place since about 1400 it is easy to realize what a vast and varied quantity of medieval music must still exist, even making allowance for a generally slower rate of change and for a high mortality rate among manuscripts. A Goliard song and a Machaut chanson may differ as profoundly as a Bach aria and a Wolf Lied. But such immense variety is clearly a strong advantage, and one which will be appreciated more and more as a greater familiarity with the music of those times develops.

Texts

Of course the resurrection of such music for workaday use by ordinary people is not without its problems. Chief of these is the provision of suitable words. Existing texts are either in Latin, langue d'oc (Provençal), langue d'oïl (medieval French), Middle High German or Middle English. The subject matter of most of the songs is love, whether courtly, romantic or sexual, and much of the imagery precious and whimsical. Although nowadays the experts tell us that schoolboys' supposed traditional distaste for love songs and references to sweet maids, singing birds, babbling brooks, moonlight and roses is largely a myth (and certainly, few pop song texts – admittedly more down to earth – seem to offend), even so, there must be a limit to their tolerance. Another problem is posed by the uncomfortably high proportion of medieval song texts pouring lavish praise on the Virgin Mary. In this book a variety of solutions is offered; in some cases existing verse translations have, with permission, been used; in others new unrelated 'poems' in various styles have been provided, and sometimes the original text has been kept in the hope of encouraging people who use the book either to attempt medieval pronunciation occasionally or to create suitable texts of their own. In this connection it is a comfort to remember that much medieval song verse is, to put it mildly, hardly top-class poetry, and also that in the Middle Ages folk were much less rigid than we are in discriminating between the sacred and the secular. Some of the latter songs, for example, the Goliard song in this book (No. 13) and the famous *Sumer* canon, are furnished with alternative sacred texts, some are based on plainsong material, and some sacred motets contain overtly secular melodies.

In strophic songs, the words of the first stanza have been placed under the notes of the melody. Although this is the most practical course, it has been taken with some reluctance as there is a risk that the other stanzas may then tend to be neglected. It is hoped that this will not be the case, as the words of all the stanzas should fit their respective melodies equally well.

Rhythm

Another problem, and one which diminishes with the later forms of medieval notation, is that of the rhythm of the music. For example, many of the monodic (solo) songs of medieval times survive only in manuscripts which, though reasonably clear as to pitch, give little or no indication of the intended rhythm. Writing as recently as 1973, Gilbert Reaney says, 'We continue to be uncertain about the rhythm of plainsong and Troubadour song and about how to perform the lower parts of medieval motets and polyphonic songs' (*Soundings* 3, University College Cardiff). The most generally accepted solution is to apply to the melodic outline the note values of the rhythmic mode which corresponds with the poetic metre of the text to which the music is set. According, therefore, to the metre of the text concerned, the rhythm of the song may be trochaic: ♩ ♪♩ ♪ etc. (mode 1), as in No. 1 and many others; iambic: ♪♩ ♪♩ etc. (mode 2); dactylic: ♩. ♪♩ etc. (mode 3); anapaestic: ♪♪ ♩. etc. (mode 4); spondaic: ♩. ♩.etc. (mode 5); or even tribrachic: ♪♪♪ etc. (mode 6). Although, as will be seen, this practice generally leads to unrelieved 6/8 time, some authorities believe that mode 3 may be transcribed in 2/4 time (♩ ♪♪) and mode 5 in 4/4 (♩♩ etc.), so a certain amount of variety is possible. For example, both *Orientis partibus* (No. 12) and *Der Kuninc Rodolp* (No. 6) may be found, sometimes interpreted in quadruple, sometimes in triple or compound duple rhythm. Any of these is acceptable, and greater variety is thus available.

Pitch

As regards pitch, it is fortunate that many of the song melodies of this period are of limited compass and therefore quite easily adaptable to any range of voice. As such songs may be accompanied by unpitched percussion only, with an occasional drone, there need be no problems involved in transposition. If recorders or other melody instruments are used it will be advisable to consider the technical implications before deciding on transposition to another key. Several of the pieces in this book are presented in two separate keys in order to widen the range of their availability. Medieval melodies were originally written in C clef notation, and modern transcriptions use either the ordinary treble clef or the treble clef with an 'octave lower' sign, thus 𝄞. In order to avoid confusion the former is taken as standard when comparing the original pitch of the tunes with the pitch used here.

Interpretation

One of the greatest advantages of the music of this time is the variety of differing treatments which it will accept. Such music will tolerate a great deal of experiment in the manner of its performance, and widely divergent interpretations may often be regarded – with little fear of contradiction – as reasonably authentic.

Here are a few suggestions for the varied treatment of pieces in this book and elsewhere. Some of the songs will be found to be designed for solo and chorus treatment; these and perhaps others may be performed antiphonally by groups of similar or differing size. Some gain by the doubling of the melody line at the unison or octave by instruments such as recorders, or by voices or instruments at the interval of a fourth below or fifth above. Pedals or drones, single or double (a fifth apart) may sometimes be added where suitable instruments are available – and where, of course, the nature of the melody permits. Introductions, interludes and codas for instruments may be derived from the melodic material of the song, this at its humblest level involving no more than the use of the first or last phrase of the melody. Simple parts for unpitched percussion instruments may be devised in most cases. These may either mark the basic pulse, pick out the prevailing rhythmic mode or, occasionally perhaps, provide a contrasting rhythm. Experiment, and let the ear decide which result is musically the most satisfactory.

Instrumentation

Although it seems unlikely that instruments other than organ and bells were officially sanctioned for use in the church service there was certainly a wide variety available elsewhere. A good reference book on the subject (for example, Anthony Baines, *Musical instruments through the ages*, Pelican, 1961, ch. 9) will provide much more information than there is room to give here. However, some brief mention of these instruments is

Reed instrument

Pipe and tabor

Flute

Musicians, from a thirteenth-century Spanish MS

5

necessary so that the most suitable modern substitutes may be selected. The groups most likely to have been involved in medieval times are:

(a) plucked and struck string (citole, gittern, harp, lute, lyre, psaltery);
(b) bowed string (crowd [=crwth], hurdy-gurdy, rebec, vièle);
(c) double-reed wind (bagpipe, shawm, and later, cornamuse and crumhorn);
(d) fipple wind (gemshorn, pipe (with tabor), recorder).

The obvious present-day substitute for group (a) is the guitar, which may be used purely for the melodic line, or as a harmony instrument providing suitable strummed chords (generally of the 'open fifth' type, that is, without the third of the chord present) on the strong beats (or some of them) and perhaps an introduction and/or interlude.

There can be no doubt, either, of the instruments for group (b). Because some tunes are technically very simple, involving in some cases no more than five different notes, there may be an opportunity here for a relative beginner on the violin; his nasal tone may be nearer to that of a rebec than that of a more accomplished violinist! Moreover, if the part should be no more than a matter of open strings and three fingers, the intonation may be acceptable too. Or perhaps the competent player may experiment in playing nearer than usual to the bridge of his instrument.

Oboe and bassoon, the standard double-reed instruments of the present day, are not only all too rare in many schools even now; they are also, particularly in the case of the former, too smooth in tone to provide realistic substitutes for their medieval counterparts – though here again the rougher tone of a student may be a help rather than a hindrance! The sound of the humble melodica, though rather dull and soon likely to pall, may be

pressed into service if necessary. Or if really hard up, but equipped with a competent trumpeter, one might experiment with various kinds of mute. The smooth tone of the single-reed clarinet, though readily available among present-day amateurs, seems less appropriate to our notions of medieval sound, but there are those who believe that its tone may not be unlike that of the mysterious douçaine.

Recorders in their various sizes are the automatic representatives of group (d). It is worth taking some trouble over the balance of these instruments; for example, one may discover that in certain conditions the shrill clarity of a plastic descant will balance a combination of two softer-toned wooden descants, or a wooden descant and tenor played in octaves.

If a pipe, reed or even electronic organ should happen to be available, it is worth remembering that the tiny medieval portative organ was, as often as not, a secular melodic instrument, its function very different from that of the organ in more recent times.

Bass instruments for pedals and drones (don't overwork the drones!) will in all probability choose themselves, a 'cello or viola being by far the most suitable, though a trombone or bassoon (or even a convenient brass band instrument) might successfully play a tenor part.

Of the pitched percussion instruments, the glockenspiel is much more suitable than the xylophone, metallophone or chime bars. Tunable tambours can represent nakers.

There is great variety in the field of unpitched percussion, but naturally some types of instrument are more appropriate than others. Small drums, tambourines, triangles and 'Indian' cymbals can all play a useful part. It is advisable to be careful in the choice of drum; some emit a sound of unmistakable

Bagpipe

Horn *Herald's trumpet*

pitch which can be distinctly uncomfortable if it is at variance with the tonality of the music.

In most of the pieces a choice of percussion rhythms is suggested, varied to suit the pace at which you decide the music shall move. Of course these rhythms may be combined if you wish, but make sure that the contribution of the percussion department is neither too heavy nor inflexible. The weaker beats should be played lightly, and singers should almost always heavily outnumber percussion players. Don't despise the humblest but most readily available forms of percussion: hand clapping, finger snapping, foot stamping and so on, where these are appropriate – and in no danger of disturbing occupants of the next room!

Those with a limited or non-existent piano technique will be relieved to discover that in this book there is no call whatever for the piano, which is one of the relatively few instruments which can have no place at all in the medieval musical scene. It would make a poor substitute even for a psaltery; give it a well-earned rest!

The chief object in scoring medieval music should be the selection of clear, bright, un-equivocal colours (well contrasted in poly-phonic textures), not necessarily crude or strident, but devoid of that smooth sophisti-cation which one finds in the expressive playing of a modern oboist, or the lush vibrato of a skilled violinist.

Tempi and expression

The pace of these pieces is of course conject-ural and subject to individual taste; the metronome markings provided should be regarded as no more than tentative sugges-tions. Try over the pieces at different speeds until you find your ideal. No expression marks have been added; this does not mean that the expression should be neglected, but that your own should evolve as your acquaintance with the pieces develops.

Conclusion

One final plea: don't give up if you can't achieve what you feel to be authentic results; it's far better to play an estampie on flute and clarinet or a motet on violin, melodica and horn, and to help matters along with a gener-ous allowance of imagination, than to close the door on centuries of music for want of a rebec, a shawm or a psaltery. And after all, however much the scholars may debate, the sounds of recorders and human voices can't have changed so very much.

This collection is intended to open a door, to stimulate ideas and to encourage a search

Man with vièle – and two apes, from a thirteenth-century MS

for further suitable material of this period. The music may at first seem a little strange, but it would be a great pity to let yourself be daunted by that as all the pieces have already been tried out in 'ordinary' schools under normal conditions. The first step is that of experiment, along the lines suggested above, in the matter of interpretation. The second concerns texts. If the mixture of originals, translations, paraphrases and independent compositions provided here doesn't meet with approval in certain circumstances, as may well be the case at times, please don't abandon all intention of using the music; try writing a text of your own. Sit down with a pencil, a sheet of blank paper and an open mind, and see what happens. You may be pleasantly surprised! For the third, a list of sources is given to assist those who have the interest and initiative to seek out further attractive pieces for themselves. The opportunities are great for those prepared to make the effort.

1 *A la fontenele*

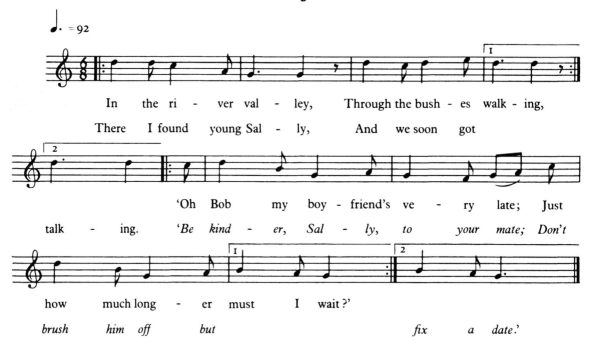

♩. = 92

In the ri - ver val - ley, Through the bush - es walk - ing,
There I found young Sal - ly, And we soon got

'Oh Bob my boy - friend's ve - ry late; Just
talk - ing. 'Be kind - er, Sal - ly, to your mate; Don't

how much long - er must I wait?'
brush him off but *fix a date.'*

2 'Gorgeous Sally, love me!
   Bob's a fool; you know it.
   And you're not above me,
   For I'm rich and show it.
   I'll give you cash and clothes for free
   If only you'll go out with me.'
   'Be kinder,' etc.

3 'Not so fast, you schemer;
   Talking smooth won't get me.
   Bob may be a dreamer,
   But he'll never fret me.
   I think he's great, so off you race
   Before I start to slap your face.'
   'Be kinder,' etc.

Original French version:

1 A la fontenele,
   Qui sourt soz la raime
   Trouvai pastorele
   Qui n'ert pas vilaine.
   Ou el se dementoit d'Amors:
   'Deus quant vendra mon ami douz?'
   'Merci, merci douce Marote,
   N'ociez pas vostré ami douz.'

Suggested drone:

 etc.

Suggested percussion parts:

Quick pace etc.   *Slow pace* etc.

Melody in a lower key:

drone:

etc.

The art of the Trouvères, the poet-musicians of northern France, flourished during the twelfth and thirteenth centuries, and about 800 of their songs have survived with words and melody complete. This anonymous song is one of the type known as the *rotrouenge,* which has two melodic phrases, the second of which is sung either once as a refrain or – as in this case – twice, the first time as part of the stanza, and the second as the refrain. It is also a *pastourelle* in that it tells the story of a knight's attempt – and failure – to seduce a young shepherdess. You will notice that the tune has no F sharps; it uses the notes of the Mixolydian mode which you can find by playing a scale of eight white notes on the piano beginning and ending on G.

The first stanza of the original poem is given here. As an exact English translation would hardly be popular in modern schools a free adaptation in more colloquial style has been provided. If you don't like it, have a try at producing a version of your own. The words of the refrain are in italic.

Guide to pronunciation

Opinions differ on this, but here are a few suggestions.

fontenele pastorele Marote	=	last e pronounced as in German Knabe
sourt	=	soort
soz	=	sots
raime	=	two syllables, the first răee and the second ending like Knabe
trouvai	=	trovay
n'ert	=	nairt
pas amors	=	the s is pronounced
vilaine	=	three syllables, the second and third as in raime above
dementoit	=	dementoyt
Deus	=	deuce
quant	=	the t is pronounced
ven(dra)	=	as in modern French vin
douz	=	doots (the ts very quiet)
n'ociez	=	not-see-ates

Horsemen hawking in May

9

2a *A l'entrade del tens clar*

♩. = 96

When the spring comes bright and clear, *Hey hoo-ray!*

Out we go with ma-ny a cheer, *Hey hoo-ray!*

Vy - ing with our com - rades here *Hey hoo-ray!*

For the tro - phies of the year In sport - ing on this

green ex - panse. *That's the life; ____ let's en - joy it!*

Come and dance; ___ now's your chance. Gai - ly prance,

leap, ca - per! Now's your chance; ____ come and dance!

2 Strong the light and warm the sun,
      Hey hooray!
Though the season's just begun.
      Hey hooray!
Now we're free, for work is done.
      Hey hooray!
Till the day its course has run
We're bursting with exuberance.
That's the life; let's enjoy it! etc.

Suggested percussion parts:

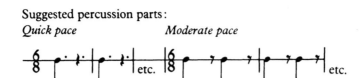

The Troubadours came from Provence in Southern France, and their art arose, flourished and died about fifty years in advance of the Trouvère art. They suffered severely in the so-called Albigensian Crusade of the early thirteenth century, but despite the bloodshed and destruction over three hundred complete songs have survived.

This is an anonymous Troubadour dance song of the type called a *ballade,* and it has two refrains: a short interjection (here translated as 'hey hooray!') in the course of the stanza, and a longer one at the end.

2b *Veris ad imperia*

When the spring comes bright and clear, Hey hoo - ray!

Out we go with ma - ny a cheer, Hey hoo-ray!

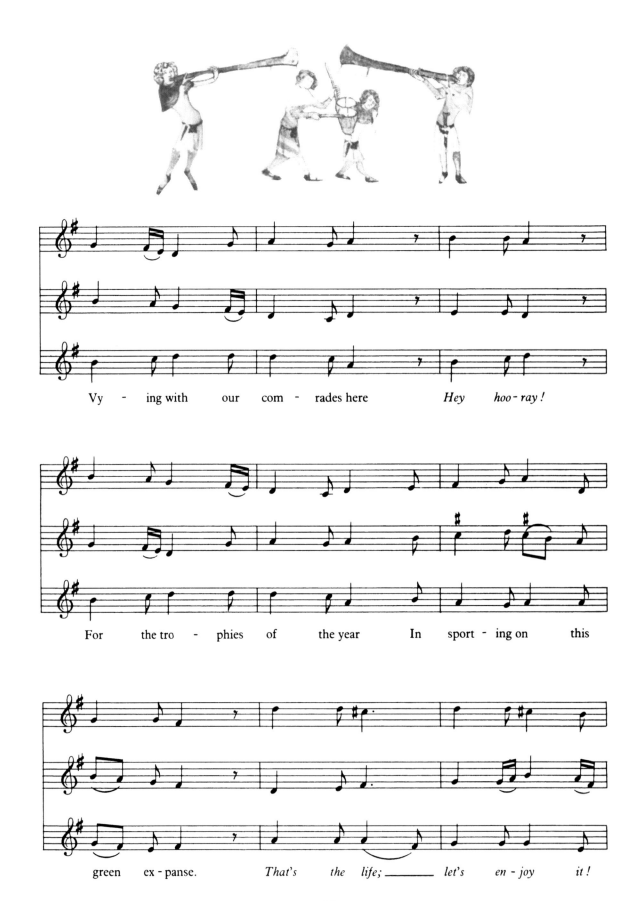

Vy - ing with our com - rades here *Hey hoo - ray!*

For the tro - phies of the year In sport - ing on this

green ex - panse. *That's the life; ——— let's en - joy it!*

Fifteenth-century Flemish (?) musicians

Come and dance; ___ now's your chance. Gai - ly prance,

leap, ca - per! Now's your chance; ___ come and dance!

The three-part version (like No. 12, best performed an octave lower) has Latin words (*Veris ad imperia renascuntur omnia:* In the reign of spring everything is reborn) and the melody is slightly different in places. The other parts may be sung or played; you'll notice that they exchange phrases. Editorial suggestions for C sharps are placed above the stave. Enjoy the discords!

3 *Au tans d'aoust*

♩ = 96

Au - tumn is com - ing; the leaves will all die,

Fall from the trees when the wind ri - ses high.

Flowers now are fad - ing and gard' - ners are spad - ing; A -

way swal - lows fly. Birds still are sing - ing and

squir - rels are spring - ing, But cold wea - ther's nigh.

2 Winter is coming; the leaves are all gone
  Down from the trees in the wind, ev'ry one.
  Flowers now have faded and gard'ners have spaded;
  Of swallows we've none.
  Birds do no singing and squirrels no springing;
  The year marches on.

Suggested guitar (or pizzicato string) accompaniment:

This is another anonymous Trouvère song, and one which is in a rather simpler style. Beware of the catch in bar 17! The original text refers to frost and leaf fall in August. Does this suggest poetic licence or a change in the weather pattern? As the tune is quite short it may be played through first, and between stanzas, on a melody instrument.

4 *Bergier de ville champestre*

Shep-herds work high in the moun-tains, tend-ing their
sheep ev'-ry day with care. Loy-al dogs rea-dy to
help them, swift-ly their mas-ter o-bey, And a-
lert, lis-ten to what he will say. They
dare all dan-gers de-fy, and if
hurt, at their work brave-ly they stay.

2 Sometimes the wolves may be lurking, seeking a chance to attack the sheep.
Flocks are with vigilance guarded, warned at the sight of a pack.
Day and night, someone must keep the wolves back.
Yet still in peace the sheep graze. Men and dogs courage and skill do not lack.

Suggested percussion part:

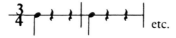 etc.

This song is by the Trouvère, Robert de Rains, and is interesting for the rather unusual rhythm in this version. A percussion part giving a note on the first beat of each bar will make the song easier to sing, and the pace should not be too slow. The first seven bars, or the last three with a final note of double length, can serve as an instrumental introduction.

5 Bergeronnete

♩. = 100

Solo or Group A

Let's ce - le - brate to - ge - ther in the mea - dow!

Come, — for to - day is St Geor - ge's —— Day.

Come, — for to - day is St Geor - ge's —— Day.

Rest or Group B

Yes, we will all come to the —— mea - dow,

There to join in games and —— danc - ing.

Solo or Group A

Eng - land's St George was a knight cou - ra - geous,

Clad all in stout and shin - ing —— ar - mour;

Slew a —— dra - gon both fierce and —— strong.

Let's ce - le - brate to - ge - ther in the mea - dow!

Come, ___ for to-day is St Geor-ge's ___ Day.

Rest or Group B

Oh ___ yes, we'll will-ing-ly join you ___ now.

Suggested percussion parts:

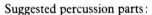

Quick pace   *Moderate pace*   *Leisurely pace*

Suggested ending:

join you   now.___

St George and the Dragon (fifteenth-century)

Adam de la Halle (*c.*1240–*c.*1286) was one of the last and greatest of the Trouvères; he composed not only solo songs, but also part-songs, plays with music and motets. In the thirteenth century, a motet was a composition for three voice parts, the lowest of which was generally borrowed from a piece of plainsong (old church melody). It was often, but by no means always, sacred music. This lively song comes from the pastoral play *Li gieus de Robin et de Marion* (The play of Robin and Marion).

The original words, a love dialogue, have little point outside the context of the play, and have been replaced. Although he may have had nothing to do with Robin and Marion, St George was certainly well known in medieval Europe, as he is said to have been seen in a vision, helping the Crusaders at the Siege of Antioch in 1098. The story of his fight with a dragon is a medieval legend. St George's Day is celebrated on 23 April.

In this and some other pieces in the book an effective ending may be contrived by extending the last note of the melody until an extra percussion note has been sounded, as shown above.

6 *Der Kuninc Rodolp*

♩ = 69

King Ru - dolph loves Al - might - y God, his faith - ful - ness ne'er
King Ru - dolph judg - es right - eous - ly and hates de - ceit - ful

break - ing; King Ru - dolph has re - sist - ed well ma - ny a
speak - ing; King Ru - dolph's brave and vir - tuous deeds de -

de - vil - ish temp - ta - tion.
serve our ad - mir - a - tion. King Ru - dolph ho - nours

God and ev' - ry __ maid of no - ble bear - ing; King Ru - dolph oft re -

veals him - self in __ ac - tions fine and dar - ing. I

wish, in mea - sure of his wealth, that __ he may get his __

due, _____ For when the min - strels play or sing, he __

glad - ly hears, but gives them not a __ sou*! _____

* A small French coin

18

Suggested drone:

etc.

Suggested percussion parts:

Quick pace　　　　　　*Moderate pace*

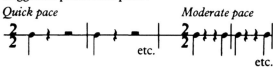

etc.　　etc.

Alternative rhythm:

etc.

German version:

Der kuninc Rodolp mynnet got und ist an
　　　　　　　　truwen stete,
Der kuninc Rodolp hat sich manigen
　　　　　　　　scanden wol vürsaget.
Der kuninc Rodolp richtet wol und hazzet
　　　　　　　　valsche rete,
Der kuninc Rodolp ist ein helt an tugenden
　　　　　　　　unvürtzaget.
Der kuninc Rodolp eret got und alle werde
　　　　　　　　vrouwen,
Der kuninc Rodolp let sich dick'in hoen
　　　　　　　　eren scouwen.
Ich gan ym wol, daz ym nach syner milte
　　　　　　　　heil gescicht,
Der meister syngen, gigen, sagen daz hort
　　　　　　　her gern und git yn drumme nicht.

The Minnesingers were the German equivalent of the Trouvères, and most of them came from the south – the area we would call Austria. This satirical song about King Rudolph I (1218-91), the first Habsburg Emperor (who seems to have been most ungenerous to his musicians) is by the wandering thirteenth century Minnesinger who called himself Der Unvürzaghete, 'The Dauntless One'. In some collections the song will be found transcribed in compound time, beginning as shown above.

Pronunciation: In medieval German, single vowel sounds are normally short, and *ou* corresponds with the modern German *au*. *W* and *st* are pronounced as in English. Nouns are written without initial capitals.

King Rudolph I, from a window in St Stephen's Cathedral, Vienna

19

7 Dy mynne ist gut

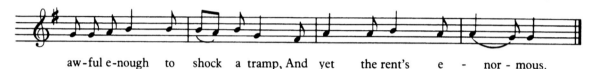

My cot-tage is damp; it gives me cramp. I'd al-most ra-ther go and camp. It's aw-ful e-nough to shock a tramp, And yet the rent's e - nor - mous.

2 The windows are cracked, and that's a fact;
The shed with broken glass is stacked.
Not even the chimney's still intact,
And yet the rent's gigantic.

3 The roof's full of leaks; the door-knob squeaks.
The drain outside the kitchen reeks.
I haven't been warm and dry for weeks,
And yet the rent's colossal.

4 Bone-dry is the pump; the floor's a sump.
The plaster falls and makes me jump.
You wouldn't believe it's such a dump,
And yet the rent's fantastic.

Suggested drone:

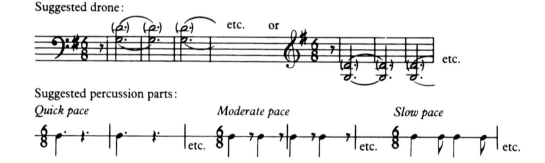

Suggested percussion parts:

Quick pace   *Moderate pace*   *Slow pace*

The German *Leich,* like the French *lai,* consists of a series of more or less independent sections strung together to make a song. The excerpt here is the ninth section of a *Leich* by the thirteenth century Minnesinger Reinmar von Zweter, who is said to have been blind. He was born about 1200, grew up in Austria and spent some years at the court of King Wenzel in Bohemia. He died about 1260. As the original song text is rather abstract a new one, less solemn in tone, is provided.

A fourteenth-century cottage in Berkshire

8 Nu huss!

♩ = 108

'At - tack!' said Sir Mi - chael of Wol - ken - stein; 'Let's

get them all!' roared Os - wald of Wol - ken - stein; 'Let fly!' cried Sir Leo - nard of

Wol - ken - stein, 'From Grei - fen - stein we'll soon send them quick - ly on their way.'

2   We then made the fire-bearing missiles fall
On Fred'rick's men attacking the castle wall
And blaze on their armour and helmets all;
Discarding them they fled in their hopeless
disarray.

3   Their tents, heavy weapons and great fire
shield
Were quickly burned to ash in the upper field.
I'm told evil deeds evil wages yield,
And thus we're very happy to give the
Duke his pay.

Suggested percussion parts:

Quick pace   *Moderate pace*

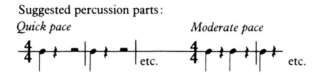

etc.   etc.

Oswald von Wolkenstein (1377-1445) was one of the last and most distinguished of the Minnesingers. He was an ambitious, avaricious and aggressive man, whose eventful life took him as far afield as Africa, Persia, Russia and Spain – a remarkable amount of travel for those days, even though some politicians and military men did move about a great deal despite the dangers and difficulties.

In 1418 Duke Friedrich II of Austria ceased to be recognized as a ruler under the Holy Roman Empire, and as a result of this he faced a rebellion on the part of the nobility of the Tyrol. Although the uprising was a failure, the defence of Greifenstein Castle near Bolzano against the Duke's troops was successful, and this song sets a part of the poem which describes the battle.

Don't allow yourself to be put off by the rather unexpected notes in this little tune, which is in the Phrygian mode. Once you are used to them you may well enjoy them.

9 Foy porter

Don't be stern When you dis-cern I'm sing - ing still ____ With a will. Though you don't thrill But rag - ing burn, Let ____ me ____ war - ble on un - til The song I learn.

[1, 2, 3 & 4]

[Last time] [Fine] **B**

learn. ____ I con -

And though ____ fess I'm short of cash, So I'm forced to cut ____ a

you may think it trash, It is o - ver in ____ a

[1] dash To get a loan.

[2] D.C.

flash, So please don't moan.

A2 You may groan –
The song's my own.
I may be rash,
Very brash,
But I don't drone;
Superb my tone.
Now your teeth don't need to gnash –
I'm nearly blown!

Repeat A1

B2 Soon I'll have enough to pay
All my debts and then go gay,
So wait till then.
I'm still hoping that the day
Will come soon, and come it may;
Don't ask me when.

22

A3 Many men
Prefer the pen;
I'd rather they
Sang, I'd say.
I won't delay,
But sing again.
Oh please don't rush off, I pray,
But say amen.

Repeat A1

Percussion part

 etc. throughout.

Perhaps the greatest composer in the whole long period of medieval music is the Frenchman Guillaume de Machaut (*c*.1300–*c*.1377). Like many educated men of medieval times Machaut was a priest, but this did not restrict his work to the inside of a church. He was secretary to King John of Bohemia whose warlike campaigns took him to many parts of Europe. Later he was employed by Charles, King of Navarre, and then successively by the kings of France and Cyprus. He ended his life as a canon in the cathedral town of Rheims, little more than twenty miles from Machaut, his presumed birthplace.

Machaut was a distinguished poet as well as composer, priest and politician. He left a certain amount of church music, but much more in the way of secular songs of various kinds. This example, one of his simpler, *monodic* (single voice-part) pieces, is a *virelai*, a song of dance origin with a recurring refrain melody.

Guillaume de Machaut rising from his chair to greet visitors

10 *Fulget hodie*

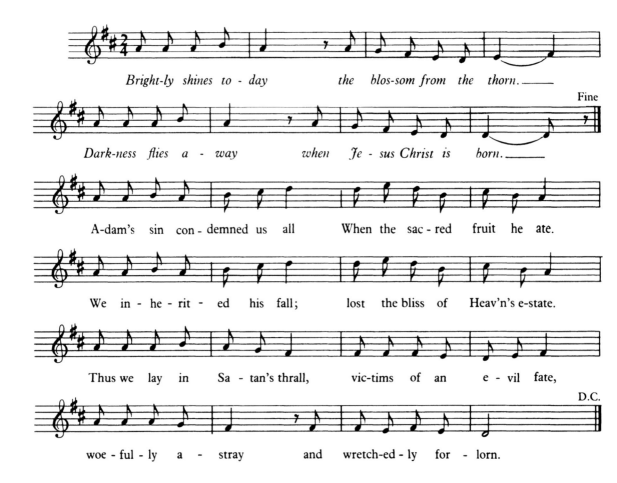

Bright-ly shines to - day the blos-som from the thorn.____

Dark-ness flies a - way when Je - sus Christ is born.____

A-dam's sin con - demned us all When the sac - red fruit he ate.

We in - he - rit - ed his fall; lost the bliss of Heav'n's e-state.

Thus we lay in Sa - tan's thrall, vic-tims of an e - vil fate,

woe - ful - ly a - stray and wretch-ed - ly for - lorn.

2 God the Father saw man's plight,
Misery and torment sore.
Though in God's image bright,
Yet the weight of sin He bore.
So to break the Devil's might,
Jesus Christ was sent to draw
All men to His sway, and came on Christmas morn.

3 Mary, Jesu's mother mild,
Laid Him in a manger bare.
She was young and undefiled;
He was innocent and fair.
Faithful Joseph gently smiled,
Keeping guard beside the pair,
Christians, all be gay at light of love's new dawn.

Suggested drone:

Suggested percussion part:

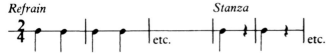

This gay and lively little carol comes from the fourteenth century. The original text is *macaronic*, that is, in a mixture of Latin and the vernacular (the language of the ordinary people) – in this case French with hints of Italian about it. Perhaps the best known of *macaronic* carols is the German *In dulci jubilo*.

11 *Omnes gentes, plaudite*

♩. = 92

All you peo - ple, clap your hands;
Praise the Lord through-out all lands. Hymn God's power which

firm - ly stands. He suf - fered sore but ·o'er us reigns.

Praise the Lord through-out all lands; His sac - ri - fice our wor - ship gains.

2 Though fulfilling God's commands,
   Praise the Lord throughout all lands.
   Crucified by cruel hands,
   He cleanses men of all their stains.
   Praise the Lord throughout all lands;
   We profit by His grievous pains.

3 Mortal and angelic bands,
   Praise the Lord throughout all lands.
   See, His influence expands
   And man's lost freedom He regains.
   Praise the Lord throughout all lands;
   He clears the way to Heaven's domains.

Latin version:

1 Omnes gentes, plaudite,
   Regi passo, psallite!
   Hymnum Deo dicite,
   Victus est qui nos vicerat;
   Regi passo, psallite,
   Passus, vicit, et imperat.

Suggested percussion parts:

Moderate pace   *Slow pace*

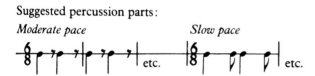 etc.   etc.

ending

There are two kinds of *rondellus*. One type is written for voices in harmony and is said to be *polyphonic*. The other kind, of which this song is an example, is for solo voice or voices in unison, and is described as *monodic*. The term *rondellus* is merely the Latin equivalent of the French *rondeau*, the Italian *rondo* and the English *round* although each of these has come to be applied to a different type of music. In this kind of *rondellus* the same opening phrase of melody keeps on recurring (or coming *round*) in a single-line tune, not in the harmony of the traditional round. One Latin stanza is retained.

12 *Orientis partibus*

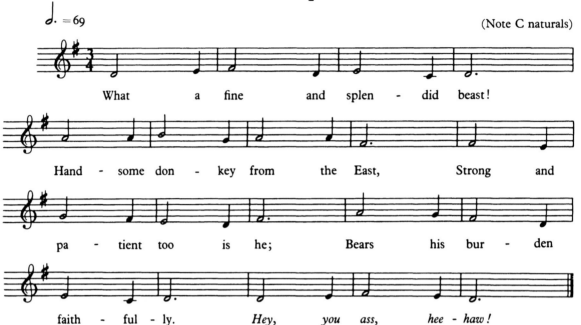

♩. = 69   (Note C naturals)

What a fine and splen - did beast!

Hand - some don - key from the East, Strong and

pa - tient too is he; Bears his bur - den

faith - ful - ly. *Hey, you ass, hee - haw!*

2 Greeting, shaggy donkey grey!
  Patiently you trudge all day.
  As you amble through the sand
  Brays resound across the land.
    Hey, you ass, hee-haw!
    (*sung after each stanza*)

3 Sturdy son of toil is he;
  Gamely plods through scrub and scree,
  Long-eared quadruped in thrall,
  Yet the chief of donkeys all.

4 As the heavy cart he draws
  Exercises he his jaws.
  Fodder crisp he masticates;
  While he chews he meditates.

5 Barley is his favourite lunch;
  Thistles, too, he loves to munch.
  When he threshes grain, his feet
  Separate the chaff and wheat.

6 Slowly dragged his weary feet
  Till he felt the lash's beat.
  Then the goad provoked his rump,
  Causing him to start and jump.

7 Reared in Sychem's hills, and fed
  Well by Reuben's tribe, he sped
  Through the River Jordan's ford;
  Bethlehem he soon explored.

8 He outleaped in his career
  Ev'ry goat, and ev'ry deer
  He ran rings around. His speed
  Stole the dromedaries' lead.

9 From Arabia gold unpriced,
  Frankincense sublimely spiced,
  Bitter myrrh from Sheba: these
  Into church he bore with ease.

10 Donkey, though you're full of hay,
  Utter forth a lusty bray.
  Bray superbly yet again;
  Spurn all vice with might and main.

11 Coarsely though you bray and long,
  Blithe, not cynical your song.
  So you'll have your just reward:
  Commendation from your Lord.

Alternative rhythm:

etc.

Suggested drone:

or

Suggested percussion parts:

Moderate pace	Slow pace	Very slow pace

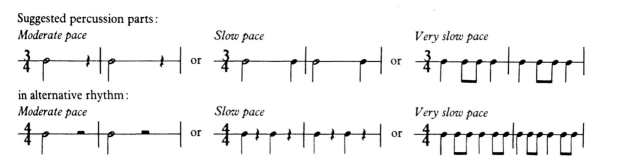

in alternative rhythm:

Moderate pace	Slow pace	Very slow pace

This famous song has already appeared in so many books that its presence in this one should perhaps be explained. There are two reasons. In the first place, although it is such a splendid processional piece one rarely sees it printed with all the available verses. Secondly, the three-part version, less well known, is also included here (p. 28).

The legends surrounding *Orientis partibus* have been told so often that one hesitates to repeat them. Suffice it to say that the song is said to have been used as an accompaniment to a procession through the French town of Beauvais, in which a young girl rode into the Cathedral on a donkey to represent the Holy Family's flight into Egypt (although parts of the text seem to suggest otherwise). According to one historian the procession took place on the first day after the Octave of the Three Kings (presumably 14 January); another asserts that it was on the day of the Circumcision (1 January). The piece seems to have been well known and widely used, and it is found in several twelfth and thirteenth century sources. Some medieval Latin songs were called *conductus*, probably because they were used while a priest was being 'conducted' from one part of the church to another.

To provide for a really long procession the tune may be played on recorder(s) between each pair of sung stanzas. It may be performed in either 3/4, 4/4 or 6/8 time. In the three-part version the two upper parts were, in the opinion of some experts, probably played on instruments. If possible all three parts should be sung and/or played in the same octave, so that the correct harmony is retained.

The Holy Family's flight into Egypt (thirteenth-century)

27

(12 continued)

Three-part version (note C sharps).
This should sound more authentic performed an octave lower.

What a fine and splen - did beast! Hand - some don - key

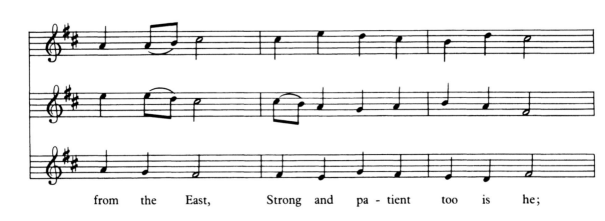

from the East, Strong and pa - tient too is he;

Bears his bur - den faith - ful - ly. *Hey, hey, you ass, hee - haw!*

Melody in a higher key:

Drones:

Part of 'Orientis partibus' in a thirteenth-century manuscript

13 *O Roma nobilis*

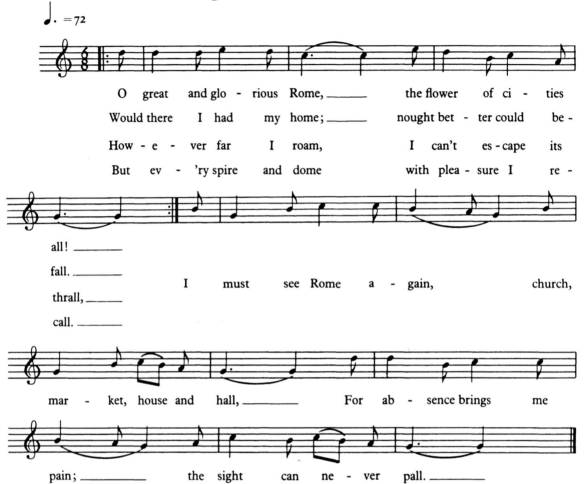

♩. = 72

O great and glo - rious Rome, ___ the flower of ci - ties
Would there I had my home; ___ nought bet - ter could be -
How - e - ver far I roam, I can't es - cape its
But ev - 'ry spire and dome with plea - sure I re -

all! ___
fall. ___ I must see Rome a - gain, church,
thrall, ___
call. ___

mar - ket, house and hall, ___ For ab - sence brings me

pain; ___ the sight can ne - ver pall. ___

2 O city past compare, as gracious as a queen!
Was ever place so fair, so awe-inspiring seen?
Such beauty, I declare, creates a mood serene;
I find a haven there from all that's vile and mean.
I must to Rome return; temptation waxes keen.
To go again I burn; let no-one intervene.

Latin version:

O Roma nobilis orbis et domina,
Cunctarum urbium excellentissima.
Roseo martyrum sanguine rubea,
Albis et liliis virginum candida;
Salutem dicimus tibi per omnia,
Te benedicimus: Salve per secula!

Suggested guitar (or pizzicato string) accompaniment:

Melody in a lower key:

Suggested accompaniment:

Goliards were students who roamed Europe in the eleventh and twelfth centuries, before universities became residential. The words of the songs they sang as they begged their way from place to place are sometimes beautiful, sometimes crude, and the tunes are generally impossible to decipher.

Of the very few that can still be performed this is the best known. Two texts survive with the tune, and both are in Latin. One is clearly a love song and the other – an alternative text which was called a *contrafactum* – is this pilgrim song in praise of Rome. The first four bars are sung four times. You may care to make up another stanza.

A procession of fifteenth-century pilgrims in Spain

14 *Prendés i garde*

I'm af-ter trout now; Keep-ers are out now. When they're a-bout, now Tip me the wink.

2 Keep a look out now!
Give me a shout now
When they're about, now
Tip me the wink.

3 Quick falls the night now;
I'm out of sight now.
Fish start to bite now
Down in the stream.

Repeat Stanza 2

4 Undergrowth's dense now
This side the fence now.
Need not be tense now,
Poaching again.

Repeat Stanza 2

5 Keepers are gone now;
I'll linger on now.
Hope to catch one now;
Supper time's here.

Repeat Stanza 1

Suggested drone:

etc.

Suggested percussion part:

etc.

This short and simple, but very rhythmic *rondeau* is one of the *monodic* type (see the note on No. 11). It was composed by Guillaume d'Amiens, a thirteenth century Trouvère. The ornament in bar 2 is better omitted if the pace is brisk. The words printed in Roman type may be sung solo or by a small group; those in italic by everyone.

Guillaume d'Amiens

15 Quand je voi

When win-ter winds come on a-pace I seek a warm and
I look for one where I can face A good square meal and

com-fy place. The sort of inn I have in mind So
leave no trace. Makes sure I've well and tru-ly dined,

that my sto-mach is well lined, Yet wants no cash of a-ny kind!

2 I also want a feather bed,
   Soft pillows for my heavy head,
   A roaring fire with logs well fed
   That's blazing bright and glowing red,
   A girl who will my spirits cheer
   And bring me lots of foaming beer.
   Please tell me if you chance to hear
   Of any such apartment near.

Suggested drone:

etc.

Suggested percussion parts:

Moderate pace   *Slow pace*

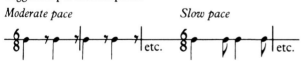

ending:

Jongleurs (or Gaukler) were minstrels, elocutionists, entertainers, jugglers, acrobats or a combination of any or all of these. They travelled from place to place, performing for what they could get in the shape of money, gifts, food or hospitality. Sometimes a Troubadour or Trouvère in straitened circumstances would be reduced to 'going on the road' as a jongleur, and conversely a cultured and successful jongleur might occasionally aspire to the company of Troubadours or Trouvères. Such 'promotion' seems to have been the case with Colin Muset (thirteenth century), to whom this song is attributed. Notice the simple, neat and economical structure of the tune.

16 *Qui creavit coelum*

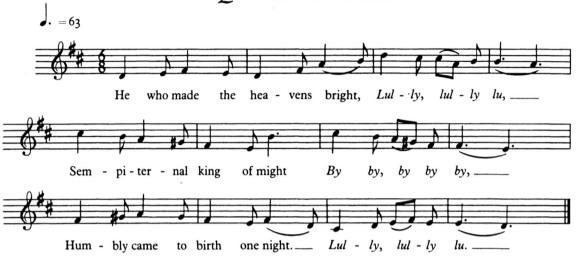

He who made the hea - vens bright, *Lul - ly, lul - ly lu,* ____

Sem - pi - ter - nal king of might *By by, by by by,* ____

Hum - bly came to birth one night. ____ *Lul - ly, lul - ly lu.* ____

2 Joseph went and bought a shawl;
        By by, by by by,
Mary wrapped the infant small,
        Lully, lully lu,
Laid him in a cattle stall.
        By by, by by by.

3 Animals stood round the child,
        Lully, lully lu,
Patient ox and donkey mild.
        By by, by by by,
As they stared the baby smiled.
        Lully, lully lu.

4 Full of awe and holy joy,
        By by, by by by,
Free from blemish or alloy,
        Lully, lully lu,
Mary fed and nursed the boy.
        By by, by by by.

5 Give us, holy child and fair
        Lully, lully lu,
In your love and grace a share.
        By by, by by by,
We will follow anywhere.
        Lully, lully lu.

6 Fill us to the very core
        By by, by by by,
With such love that, evermore
        Lully, lully lu,
We shall serve you and adore.
        By by, by by by.

Suggested part for triangle or Indian cymbals:

A processional (a book of instructions for church services) dated about 1425, belonging to the Benedictine nunnery of St Mary in Chester, contains this simple, gentle lullaby. It may be sung antiphonally, that is, by a soloist or group singing the stanza lines and a second group the refrain lines. The melody as it appears in the book is in plainsong (that is, free rhythm) notation, and so the song may be sung that way instead of in 6/8 rhythm, although it is much more difficult to do so. Alternatively the stanza lines may be sung in free rhythm (perhaps by a solo voice) and the refrain lines in 6/8.

17 *Veníte a laudáre*

♩ = 76

O come with prai-ses ring-ing, And with love to her sing-ing, Lov-ing vir-gin, maid of Da-vid's ci-ty. 1. O Ma-ry thou art glo-rious and bless-ed; Be thou e-ter-nal-ly prai-sed. I pray that thy voice for me be rai-sed Un-to thy son, maid of pi-ty.

Fine

D.C. al fine

2 O gracious Mary, listen and hear me;
Bring consolation to cheer me.
I pray for thy presence ever near me;
Swiftly respond to my ditty.

The original Italian for stanza 1 *is:*

Veníte a laudáre,
Per amóre cantáre
L'amorósa vérgene María.
María gloriósa beáta,
Sémpre sía mólto laudáta:
Preghiám ke ne si'avocáta
Al tuo fíliol, vírgo pía.

Suggested percussion part:

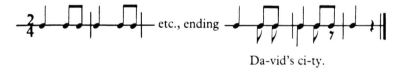

etc., ending

Da-vid's ci-ty.

During the Middle Ages, particularly in the thirteenth and fourteenth centuries, war, persecution, famine and plague aroused in many people the conviction that they must do penance for the sins of mankind. So they formed bands of pilgrims and travelled from shrine to shrine often singing songs of praise called *Laude Spirituali*. The cult of Mary, the mother of Jesus, was popular in the Middle Ages, and many songs were sung in her honour. This *lauda* is one, and like many others it was probably used by pilgrims as a marching song.

18 *Winder wie ist nu dein kraft*

Win - ter, gone is all your power! Spring, now burst-ing in - to flower,
Va - nished are the ice and snow; Mild - er winds be - gin to blow.

Drea - ri - ness will soon de - vour, Back to life all rais - ing.
Farm - ers, pon - d'ring what to sow, Pen - sive - ly stand gaz - ing.

Woods are ring - ing With the sing - ing Birds are fling - ing Through the air,
Child - ren spright - ly, laugh - ing bright - ly, Ca - per light - ly, Free from care.

See, the buds sprout forth a - new; Leaves and shoots break in - to view.
There - fore, Win - ter, bow to Spring, For of sea - sons he is king.

Vi - vid green is now the hue; Sun - shine bright is blaz - ing.
He en - li - vens ev - 'ry - thing, Con - quer - or a - maz - ing!

Suggested guitar (or pizzicato string) accompaniment:

Alternative percussion part:

Suggested drone:

Some of the songs of the Minnesingers are set to simple, unaffected tunes which may very possibly be folk melodies borrowed for use with the poems the Minnesingers wrote. Here is an example by Neidhart von Reuenthal, who was born about 1190, sang at the court of Duke Ludwig I of Bavaria, took part in a crusade and later settled in Austria, where he seems to have been in the service of the nobleman, Otto von Lengenbach. One can understand the enthusiasm with which medieval poets greeted the annual return of the spring when one stops to think how grim their life must have been in winter time.

Suggestions for further activities

Collections of music

Baines, Francis (ed.), *Dances from the Middle Ages,* London, Schott, 1965.

This is a collection of five pieces (six in fact, as one is in two contrasted sections) for descant or tenor recorder solo (or recorders in unison) with an added drum part. The music is useful and interesting for players with a fair degree of competence.

Dart, Thurston (ed.), *Invitation to medieval music,* 2 Vols. London, Stainer & Bell, 1967 and 1969.

Each of these two volumes contains a good graded selection of nineteen compositions for various combinations of voices and instruments by fifteenth-century musicians. The pieces represent a variety of subjects and styles, and range in standard from easy to fairly difficult, either technically or rhythmically. The song texts are the originals, and 'rough' translations are provided.

Davison, Archibald T., and Willi Apel (eds.), *Historical anthology of music,* Vol. 1. Cambridge, Massachusetts, Harvard University Press, rev. ed., 1949.

This invaluable collection of over 180 pieces covers the main streams of musical art from 1000 B.C. to the end of the sixteenth century. About fifty come under the medieval umbrella. Translations of the original texts and notes on each item are provided.

Dunston, Ralph, and Christopher Bygott, *Songs of the ages,* Huddersfield, Schofield & Sims, rev. ed., 1962.

The first edition (referred to in the Introduction to this collection) was called *Musical Appreciation through Song.* Admirable as it was as a work which pioneered the use of medieval music in schools, it suffered inevitably from the shortcomings of its time, and the 1962 revision by Frederick Westcott sets out to remedy those defects. The medieval section has been revised and expanded and the explanatory notes have been pruned and partly rewritten. The songs have English texts, though these may not all be to the taste of modern boys and girls. For those who want them, some of the piano accompaniments from the earlier edition have been retained.

Gennrich, Friedrich (ed.), *Troubadours, Trouvères, Minnesang and Meistergesang* Anthology of Music, Vol. 2, Köln, Arno Volk Verlag, 1960.

This volume contains some 78 medieval songs from France and Germany covering nearly 400 years, and is a happy hunting ground for anyone in search of practical material. A substantial introduction and commentary in English are provided, but there is no translation of the texts.

Gleason, Harold (ed.), *Examples of music before 1400,* New York, Appleton-Century-Crofts, 1942.

The book is an impressive selection of over a hundred pieces, ranging from Greek and Hebrew chants, through organum and secular monodic songs to motets, cacce and madrigals. Most of the old favourites are present, and although it is evident that much musicological water has flowed under the medieval bridge since the first appearance of the collection there is still a great deal to interest the seeker. The brief preface is of course in English, but the texts are all in the original languages.

Harrison, Frank Lloyd (ed.), *Now make we merthe,* 3 Vols. London O.U.P., 1968, *Two fourteenth-century carols,* London, Faber, 1968.

Between them the three slim books of *Now make we merthe* muster sixteen Christmas Carols dating from the twelfth to the sixteenth centuries, some for solo or unison voices and others polyphonic. In some cases instrumental accompaniments are provided, and the texts are translated into English at the end of each book. The carols have been recorded on Argo RG and ZRG 526. A very interesting and useful series, though rather expensive. The same comments apply to the *Two fourteenth-century carols*.

Husmann, Heinrich (ed.), *Medieval polyphony*, Anthology of Music, Vol. 9. Köln, Arno Volk Verlag, 1962.

This collection contains examples of organum, clausula, conductus, motet, caccia and madrigal, in from two to four voice parts. The introduction is in English, but the texts are all the originals. An interesting volume for the dedicated specialist, but its practical value for schools and amateurs is limited.

Ochs, Gerd (ed.), *Musik der Gotik*, Celle, Hermann Moeck Verlag, 1964.

This booklet of music for three recorders or other instruments contains six pieces covering a period of about 250 years from the time of the Notre Dame organa to that of Binchois. One of the items (the Machaut *Ballade*) does not go below (written) Middle C, and may therefore by played on three descant or tenor recorders, but the others need two descants and treble (the treble reading up an octave) or two tenors or flutes with violin or clarinet. Several of the pieces are rhythmically quite involved and may stretch – or even defeat – many an amateur musician.

Seagrave, Barbara G., and J. Wesley Thomas, *The songs of the Minnesingers*, Urbana, University of Illinois Press, 1966.

This is a substantial book (with an accompanying gramophone record) which gives valuable information on the Minnesingers, their background, their lives and their art, together with many examples of their songs. Both the original and English texts are provided. Expensive but very useful.

Thomson, John M. (ed.), *Early music*, London, Oxford University Press, 1973.

An enterprising quarterly periodical has been launched under this title. Its aim is 'to provide a link between the finest scholarship of our day and the amateur and professional listener and performer'. The adjective 'early' is interpreted liberally, and a wide range of topics is covered. The article in the first number (January 1973) on percussion instruments of the Middle Ages and Renaissance by James Blades is particularly valuable. Each issue contains a musical supplement in a practical edition.

Turner, Bruno (ed.), *Five thirteenth-century pieces*, London, Schott, 1962.

The first of these arrangements for three recorders needs a C instrument on its lowest part (unless a treble reads up an octave and plays with two descants), but the others may be played on 'equal' recorders, tenor, treble or descant, or by any convenient mixed combination, and the editor encourages the addition of string and percussion instruments. The parts are not difficult (the lowest – tenor – part is always easy, though low), but the hocket rhythm of No. 4 can raise problems.

There are also some useful medieval pieces in: Book 3 of Geoffrey Brace. *Something to sing*. Cambridge University Press, 1966.

McGrady, Richard J., *Four thirteenth-century pieces*, London, Chester, 1972 (for recorders).

The list of music sources below mentions some other collections.

Background reading

Baines, Anthony (ed.). *Musical instruments through the ages.* Harmondsworth, Middlesex, Penguin Books, 1961.

Grout, Donald Jay. *A history of western music.* London, Dent, 1962.

Harman, Alec, Wilfrid Mellers and Anthony Milner. *Man and his music.* London, Barrie and Rockliff 1962.

Harrison, Frank Lloyd. *Music in medieval Britain.* London, Routledge and Kegan Paul, 1958.

Hughes, Dom Anselm (ed.). *New Oxford history of music,* vol. II. London, O.U.P., 1954.

Hughes, Dom Anselm and Gerald Abraham (eds.). *New Oxford history of music,* vol. III. London, O.U.P., 1960.

Reese, Gustave. *Music in the Middle Ages.* London, Dent, 1941.

Reese, Gustave. *Music in the Renaissance.* London, Dent, 1954.

Robertson, Alec and Denis Stevens. *Pelican history of music,* vol. I. Harmondsworth, Middlesex, Penguin Books, 1960.

Seay, Albert. *Music in the medieval world.* Englewood Cliffs, New Jersey, U.S.A., Prentice-Hall, 1965.

Smoldon, William L. *A history of music.* London, Herbert Jenkins, 1965.

Young, Percy M. *A history of British music.* London, Benn, 1967.

The Bibliographies in *Man and his music, Music in the Middle Ages* and *New Oxford history of music* are useful.

Records

The following records include songs from this book (indicated in parentheses). The list is not necessarily complete, and new recordings appear from time to time. Some of the records have now been deleted, but may occasionally be available second hand or from lending libraries.

The art of the minstrel, Grosvenor GRS 1013 (No. 1).

The central Middle Ages, Archive APM 14018 (Nos. 2a, 5, 14).

Guillaume de Machaut, Works, Oiseau-Lyre SOL 310 (No. 9).

The history of music in sound, H.M.V. HLP 3 (Nos. 3, 5, 13 (different text), 15); HLP 4 (No. 12).

Medieval music, Pye GSGC 1 (No. 12).

Minnesong and prosody, Telefunken SAWT 9487-A Ex (No. 6)

Now make we merthe, Argo RG 526 (Nos. 10, 12).

Troubadour songs, Telefunken SAWT 9567-B (Nos. 2a, 2b).

Sources

Unless otherwise noted, English song words are by B. Sargent.

1. Music: Friedrich Gennrich, *Die altfranzösische Rotrouenge* (1925), p. 60. Transcription in Harman, Mellers and Milner, *Man and his music* (1962), Barrie & Rockliff, p. 79. Original pitch as in first version. Words: B. Sargent (English); French, as for music.

2. Music: (a) Paris, Bibl. Nat. fr. 20050, fo.82v. (b) Florence, Bibl. Laur. plut. XXIX, 1, fo.228v. Transcription (a) in A. Hughes (ed.), *New Oxford history of music*, Vol. II (1954), O.U.P., p. 241; (b) H. Gleason, *Examples of music before 1400*, (1942), Appleton-Century-Crofts Inc., p. 41.

3. Music: Paris, Bibl. Nat. fr. 846, fo.13v. Transcription in *New Oxford history of music*, vol. II, p. 232. Original a tone lower.

4. Music: 957 M.S.X. (Chans. Germ.) fol.187a. Transcription in Gennrich, *Troubadours, Trouvères, Minnesang & Meistergesang*, from *Anthology of music*, vol. II, Arno Volk, Verlag (1960), p. 37. Original a tone lower.

5. Music: Paris, Bibl. Nat. fr. 25566, fo.41. Transcription in *New Oxford history of music*, vol. II, p. 232. Original a tone lower.

6. Music: F. L. Saran, *Die Janaer Liederhandschrift*, vol. II (1902), p. 26. Transcription in *Man and his music*, p. 87. Words: as for transcription, slightly adapted. Original a tone lower.

7. Music: Vienna, Nationalbibl. 2701, fo.12. Transcription in *New Oxford history of music*, vol. II, p. 257. Original a tone lower.

8. Music: Innsbruck, Universitätsbibliothek, fo.36. Transcription in H. J. Moser, *Geschichte der deutschen Musik*, vol I, (1920), J. G. Cotta'sche Buchandlung Nachfolger. Original a tone lower.

9. Music: Paris, Bibl. Nat. fr. 843, 1586. Transcriptions in L. Schrade (ed.), *Polyphonic music of the fourteenth century*, vol. III, (1956-71) Editions de l'Oiseau Lyre; and F. Ludwig (ed.), *Guillaume de Machaut, Musikalische Werke*, vol. I, (1926-), Breitkopf & Hartel. Original a minor third higher. Both transcriptions slightly adapted.

10. Music: Transcription in F. L. Harrison, *Now make we merthe*, Book 1 (1968), O.U.P., Original a minor third higher.

11. Music: Florence, Bibl. Laur. plut. XXIX, 1, fo.465. Transcription in *New Oxford history of music*, vol. II, p. 243. Original a perfect fourth higher. Words: B. Sargent (English); Latin, as for music.

12. Music: Brit. Mus. Egerton 2615 and others. Transcriptions in *New Oxford history of music*, vol. II, pp. 174 and 321, and F. L. Harrison, *Now make we merthe*, Book 1 (1968), O.U.P., p. 2, and many others. Original pitch as in third version.

13. Music: (1) Camb. Univ. Lib. Gg.v.35, fo.441v; (2) Vatican 3327; (3) Monte Cassino, Q 318, fo.291. Transcription in *New Oxford history of music*, vol. II, p. 221. Original pitch as in first version. Words: B. Sargent (English); Latin, as for music.

14. Music: Rome, Vaticana Reg. Christ. 1490. Transcription in H. Gleason, *Examples of music before 1400* (1942), Appleton-Century-Crofts Inc., p. 9. Original a tone lower.

15. Music: Paris, Bibl. Nat. fr. 846, fo.125v. Transcription in *New Oxford history of music*, vol. II, p. 241. Original a major third lower.

16. Music: Huntington Library, San Marino, California, MS EL34, B7. Transcription in A. Hughes and G. Abraham (eds.) *New Oxford history of music*, vol. III, (1960), p. 117. Original a minor third higher.

17. Music: Thirteenth-century MS at Cor-

tona, and Fernando Liuzzi, *Melodie Italiane inedite del duocento in Archivum Romanicum* (1930), XIV. Transcription in *Man and his music*, p. 85. Original a

18. Music: Berlin, Preuss. Staatsbibl. germ. 779, fo.142. Transcription in *New Oxford history of music*, vol. II, p. 256.

Sources of illustrations

Front cover, pp. 1, 5, 6 from *Cantigas di S. Maria*, Library of the Escorial, Madrid; **p. 7** from the Tenison Psalter, British Museum MS 24686, fo. 17v; **p.9** Trinity College, Cambridge B.11.3.1; **pp. 12, 13** Luttrell Psalter, British Museum; **p. 17** Bodleian Library, Oxford MS Auct. D. inf. 2.11 fo. 44v; **p. 19** Austrian National Library Vienna; **p. 20** National Buildings Record; **p. 23** Paris, Bibliothèque Nationale, fr. 1584; **p. 27** British Museum MS 28784 B fo. 6v; **p. 29** British Museum MS Egerton 2615, fo. 43v; **p. 31** Musée Conde, Chantilly, MS 1362 fo. 95, Photograph by Giraudon; **p. 32** Vatican Library, Reg. Christ 1490 fo. 85r.

Index of Songs

A la fontenele 8
A l'entrade del tens clar 10
All you people 25
'Attack!' 21
Au tans d'aoust 14
Autumn is coming 14
Bergeronnete 16
Bergier de ville 15
Brightly shines today 24
Der Kuninc Rodolp 18
Don't be stern 22
Dy mynne ist gut 20
Foy porter 22
Fulget hodie 24
He who made the heavens 34
I'm after trout 32
In the river valley 8
King Rudolph 18
Let's celebrate together 16

My cottage is damp 20
Nu huss! 21
O come with praises ringing 35
O great and glorious Rome 30
Omnes gentes 25
Orientis partibus 26
O Roma nobilis 30
Prendés i garde 32
Quand je voi 33
Qui creavit coelum 34
Shepherds work high 15
Veníte a laudáre 35
Veris ad imperia 11
What a fine and splendid beast! 26
When the spring comes 10
When winter winds come 33
Winder wie ist nu dein kraft 36
Winter, gone is all your power! 36

Lightning Source UK Ltd.
Milton Keynes UK
UKOW020022270613

212877UK00012B/1662/P